D1109229

B O N S A I —

MINIATURE POTTED TREES

TOURIST LIBRARY

Volumes Already Published

Volumes in Preparation

Tokaede (Trident Maple). Of this miniature maple tree M. Claudel, French poet and ex-Ambassador to Japan, once remarked that he imagined himself in a maple grove, listening to the chirrups of birds in the boughs. (Page 16)

Printed by Toppan Printing Co.

Tokyo, Japan

BONSAI—

Miniature Potted Trees

BY

NORIO KOBAYASHI

JAPAN TRAVEL BUREAU
TOKYO

EDITORIAL NOTE

The purpose of the Tourist Library Series is to give to the passing tourists and other foreigners interested in Japan a basic knowledge of various phases of Japanese culture. When completed, the Series is expected to include a hundred volumes or so, and will give a complete picture of Japanese culture, old and new.

The Library was started in 1934 by the Board of Tourist Industry and was transferred to the Japan Travel Bureau in 1943, when 40 volumes had been completed.

From the beginning the Library attained a high reputation as a concise but reliable interpreter of Japanese culture, and the demand for the volumes steadily increased both in Japan and abroad. Unfortunately, however, the old volumes are out of stock. The Japan Travel Bureau, therefore, has begun a new series,—revising and reprinting some of the old volumes, and issuing others on entirely new and equally interesting subjects.

Each volume in the Library is the work of a recognized authority on the subject, and it is hoped that by perusing these studies of Japanese life the reader will gain some insight into the unique culture that has developed in this country throughout the ages.

The present volume, "Bonsai," is the work of Mr. Norio Kobayashi, who has been publishing and editing "Bonsai," which is the most influential monthly magazine on the subject in this country, since its inception

30 years ago. A former lecturer at the Tokyo College of Gardening, and one of the founders and major executives of the Kokufu Bonsai Tenrankai, the biggest bonsai exhibition annually held in this country, he is an acknowledged authority on *bonsai* in present-day Japan.

Our special thanks are due to Mr. Rokuo Okada of the Liaison Office of the Japanese National Railways who translated the original Japanese manuscript into English. We also desire to record our sincere appreciation of the help given by Dr. Hisayoshi Takeda (D.Sc., D.I.C.), who identified the English names of the trees· Finally we take pleasure in thanking Prof. Michiya Yasuda of Koryo University, who gave us many valuable suggestions in the editing of this book.

EDITOR

July, 1950.

PREFACE

Painting, sculpture and other branches of art enable us to visualize afresh the scenes and other objects, animate or inanimate, which have excited our sense of beauty in the past. But there is a living thing which goes a little farther and enables us to envisage a piece of scenery which is subject to seasonal changes, and that is what the Japanese call a "bonsai." Because of its uniqueness one can say that the art of making a bonsai is in a class by itself.

Western lovers of art and nature, who are convinced that bonsai-making is a unique art, have asked me various questions about it. And upon the request of the Japan Travel Bureau I have furnished an answer in book form as an addition to the Bureau's Tourist Library Series.

In the limited space offered by this booklet it is next to impossible to go into full details on the subject. The object of this brochure is mainly to give the reader the assurance that the bonsai is not merely a triumph of dwarfing to be wondered at, but that it is also a thing of beauty designed to take the beholder into the realms of poetry where he can see in his imagination some landscape or other as presented by Nature.

Norio Kobayashi

Nagano,
July, 1950

CONTENTS

ILLUSTRATIONS

Cover Photo :   Higan-zakura
                (Drooping Cherry)

WHAT IS A BONSAI?

The word bonsai has been and still is translated as
"dwarf tree" or "potted dwarf tree." But if the word
dwarf carries a suggestion of something stunted and out
of proportion even to the verge of deformity, then
the term "dwarf tree" is not appropriate. For, though
created by the process of dwarfing, the bonsai, as we
understand it today, should signify anything but a de-
formed potted-tree. Nor does the term "miniature tree"
convey the exact truth about the bonsai. Such an ex-
pression as "an art of cultivating a plant or a tree in a
pot" might be more felicitous. Here in this booklet,
however, the Japanese word bonsai is used throughout,
since it has already crept into the English language and
is treated under that title in such a reputable work as
the Encyclopaedia Britannica.

A bonsai is to be distinguished from an ordinary
potted plant (*hachi-ue*). In its broad sense a bonsai is
no doubt a kind of potted plant, but it definitely differs
from the latter in being a work of art, a fact which is
universally admitted. A bonsai may be defined as a
tree or trees cultivated through nanization, that is, artificial dwarfing, in a small tray-like vessel, so as to be
admired for the effect it is intended to produce,—which
is to create an aesthetic sentiment by suggesting a piece
of scenery. In contrast to this a *hachi-ue* is a plant

cultivated in a pot so as to be admired for the beauty of its flowers and leafage from a botanical point of view. So-called potted plants are appreciated merely for the verdure of their leaves and the resplendence of their flowers, whereas bonsai evoke appreciation of the beautiful by their suggestions of landscapes.

Bonsai are designed to express the beauty of nature as brought out by all sorts of phenomena imaginable. A bonsai hardly a foot in height may, for instance, conjure up an aged, giant tree or trees standing upright, now silhouetted against the moonlit sky and now sighing in the wind. Another bonsai may suggest a wide expanse of field spreading beyond the trees represented in the pot; and a third, forest or shrubbery, or an ubiquitous grove of trees amongst which nestles a Shinto shrine or a Buddhist temple. Persons of aesthetic sensibilities may even picture to themselves birds singing among the trees or insects chirping in the grass when they look at a bonsai representation of a landscape. A "cascade" bonsai, that is, a tree trained to suggest one overhanging a cliff, will bring to mind the limpid stream gurgling past below.

I remember once seeing M. Claudel, who was one-time French Ambassador to Japan, seated upright and lost in deep contemplation, in front of a maple tree treated as a bonsai. "Looking at this deciduous tree," he explained, when asked why, "I cannot help imagining myself in a maple grove. I feel as if as I were hearing the chirrups of birds in the boughs." These words expressed his sentiments on that occasion. Like the

Hinoki
(Hinoki Cypress)

Photographed in July
Height: 2 ft. 3 in.

Shimpaku (Chinese Juniper)
with two trunks growing
from one stump

Photographed in winter
Height: 1 ft. 7 in.

poet that he was, he expressed an aesthetic appreciation of a bonsai.

There is a Lilliputian form of poetry which the Japanese call *haiku*. Composed of but seventeen syllables, it is instrumental in expressing all sorts of sentiments born of seasonal changes. It aims at expressing the maximum of poetic feeling with the minimum of words. In this sense the bonsai and the *haiku* have something in common. It may be that the people of this small island country evolved, before they were aware of it, this method of embracing much in little, while leading a life of privation and perseverance.

Love of Nature knows no tedium. Even a blade of grass unfamiliar to the general run of people has its season and gives us delight. Different field grasses have different characteristics according to the setting in which they grow. A bonsai bears the stamp of the individuality of each plant so cultivated; it is intended to bring out its characteristic or characteristics so conspicuously as to touch the chord of aesthetic sentiment.

A bonsai differs from a *bonkei* (tray-landscape) whose function is also to represent a landscape, because the latter does not involve the cultivation of plants. The aim of a *bonkei* is to reproduce a landscape as artistically as practicable on a tray: it makes no difference whether the artist uses animate or inanimate things to work on. The landscape thus presented does not breathe; it does not reveal seasonal charms in the same way as does the scenery suggested by a bonsai. The art of making bonsai involves in itself the pleasure of cultivating trees;

the sort of gratification which a mother finds in bringing up her child. It is accomplished with affection. To show affection is to comfort oneself. Herein lies the distinctive feature of the art of nurturing trees in tray-pots.

Shidare-zakura (Drooping Cherry)

Kaede (Maple)

Photographed in winter
Height: 1 ft. 8 in.

~21

Yamazakura (Mountain Cherry)

THE HISTORY OF BONSAI

We find the oldest record of bonsai in some of the picture scrolls (*emakimono*)* dating from the beginning of the thirteenth century. These scrolls illustrated the miraculous effect of prayers offered at the Kasuga shrine** in Nara and the principal events in the life of the priest Honen Shonin (1133–1212), founder of the Jodo sect of Buddhism. Here we see pictures of trees or grasses transplanted from the outdoors in shallow pots as garden ornaments. This way of admiring plants in those far-off days, despite the fact that planting flowers and trees in a garden had already become a custom, shows the appreciation of the beautiful as expressed in the form of bonsai. Then in the fifteenth century, which is known as the Muromachi period in Japanese history, there is found another reference to bonsai in the famous No play entitled *Hachi-no-Ki* or "The Potted Trees," showing that even in those days the people loved to cultivate in pots such trees as the pine, the Japanese apricot and the cherry. In this play Sano Genzaemon, a penniless but nevertheless warm-hearted and faithful samurai, makes fuel of his favorite potted-pine to warm

---

* "Japanese Fine Arts" by T. Sagara, Tourist Library No. 9, pp. 54-78.
** "How to See Kansai Area," published by the Japan Travel Bureau, pp. 80-81.

A Kokufu Bonsai Exhibition at the Ueno Art Gallery

his guest on a cold, snowy night, a guest who proves to be a *shogun* traveling incognito.

It was about a century ago that the word bonsai became popular among the painters and poets of the time. But in those days the general tendency was to set store by bonsai which represented rugged, gnarled, fantastic trees; trees dwarfed even to grotesque misproportion. The true motive of the art of making bonsai was thus lost sight of, but, fortunately, this unnatural interest in "crippled" trees gradually disappeared.

In recent years—in 1928 to be more precise—a grand bonsai exhibition was held in Hibiya Park, Tokyo. On that occasion fine specimens were collected from various parts of the country. Similar shows took place several times in succession. Then in the year 1934 there were two exhibitions of first-class bonsai, triumphs of nanization, given at the Art Gallery in Ueno Park, once in spring and once in autumn. These Ueno exhibitions, known as the Kokufu Bonsai Exhibitions, became annual events, suspended by the outbreak of the Pacific War, but resumed in 1947.

Example of bonsai art displayed at
a Kokufu Bonsai Exhibition

CLASSIFICATION BY SHAPE AND FORM

Bonsai are cultivated to increase one's appreciation of trees in their natural state. Therefore it is only natural that different bonsai should have different shapes. Bonsai are classified according to the number and shape of their trunks.

Classified by Shape of Trunk

1. *Chokkan* (Upright Trunk). As its name indicates, this type of bonsai represents a tall tree standing erect in level country, lording it over the shrubbery around. If a sapling shows vigorous growth, a mature tree produces an impression of sublimity.

2. *Shakan* (Slanting Trunk). This name is given to a bonsai representing a tree growing at right angles to a slope. The foliage of such a tree is generally thicker on the side facing the sun. A bonsai with this type of trunk is sometimes called *han-kengai* (semi-cascade).

3. *Hankan* (Gnarled and Twisted Trunk). This suggests the stunted trunk of a tree growing on top of a cliff or a wind-swept crag.

4. *Kengai* (lit. Overhanging a Cliff; Drooping Trunk). A tree rooted in a crevice on a cliff is liable to droop its upper part. A "cascade" bonsai represents such a tree looking down on a gorge.

Right: G o y o -
m a t s u (Five-
needled Pine)—
An example of
the *Kengai* style

Below: N e z u
and K a t a h i b a
cultivated on a
stone

Left: Keyaki
(Keaki)—An Ex-
ample of the
Chokkan style

Below; Ezo-
matsu (Yesso
Spruce) in the
Shakan style

Above : Ezo-matsu (Yesso Spruce) with three trunks growing
   from one stump
Below : Shimpaku (Chinese Juniper) in the *ne-tsuranari* style

Above: Sugi and Keyaki planted together in one pot
Below: Momiji in the *Kabudate* style

Classified by Number of Trunks

1. *Kabumono* is the name given to a bonsai with two or more trunks growing from one stump. When two trunks are growing in this manner, it is called *sokan* (two trunks). When there are three trunks, the plant is called *sankan* (three trunks), and when there are five, the plant is called *gokan* (five trunks). No bonsai is cultivated with four trunks. A bonsai of this kind having more than six trunks is called *kabudate* (many trunks).

2. *Yose-ue* (Trunks Planted Together). This name is used when more than two trees are cultivated in a pot. According to the number of trees, we have the names *nihon-yose* (lit. two trunks planted together), *gohon-yose* (five trunks planted together) and so on. Sometimes trees of the same kind are planted together, and sometimes different kinds of trees are put together.

3. *Ne-tsuranari* (lit. Roots Connected). In this type of bonsai several trunks shoot up, as in the case of a *yose-ue*, but from the same root which twists about the ground. In some cases, several trunks branch off upright not from a crawling root but from a recumbent trunk. This is technically known as *ikada-buki* (raft-like).

4. *Ishi-tsuki* (lit. With a Stone). This represents a tree growing on a rock. Whereas a *kengai* expresses a tree overhanging a cliff, an *ishi-tsuki* shows realism in a scene by growing out of a stone. In this type effort is made to have the roots of the tree cling around a rough stone or to plant the tree in the depression of a stone. Thus the tree and the stone combine to produce the desired effect.

Any kind of tree or any group of trees, as it appears in any landscape, can be represented by any of the types classified above. One drawback of a *yose-ue* bonsai, that is, when trees are planted in clusters, is the difficulty of keeping all the trees equally healthy for a considerable length of time. But this drawback can be eliminated, as a rule, in a *kabumono*, that is, when a tree is planted in such a way that several trunks shoot up from one stump.

With regard to *ne-tsuranari* and *ikada-buki* (raft-like), fine specimens are to be found in their natural state, and so today we have quite a number used in bonsai. There may be several factors responsible for such forms of trunks. For example, when a young and tender tree gets pinned under snow or debris and remains alive in that condition, its trunk not infrequently becomes so shaped. Bonsai makers find delight in seeking such materials to work upon.

TRUNKS, BRANCHES, LEAVES
AND ROOTS

Let us now consider the importance of the trunk, the branches, leaves and roots of a tree in the making of a bonsai. All these parts combine to make a harmonious whole in a tree. Lack of harmony among them spoils the appearance of a tree.

TRUNKS

The trunk constitutes a basis for any form of a tree, large or small. Consequently it is the keynote of one's taste in bonsai. If a bonsai is basically to represent a large tree growing in its natural state, how do we achieve the desired effect? The answer is to attach sufficient importance to the trunk. Time was when bonsai makers, in an effort at exaggeration, used to take an immense delight in creating short and stout trunks, altogether out of proportion to the stature of the tree. Hence, the general tendency was once for people to admire trees dwarfed even to monstrosity. Some exaggeration is inevitable, no doubt, in a bonsai, but the general rule today is to train a tree so as to keep both trunk and branches in proportion.

A bonsai with too slender a trunk is no more orthodox than one whose trunk is too stout and short proportionally for its height. The method of bending the

Tokaede (Trident Maple)—A miniature replica of a giant
tree standing alone in the fields

trunks to such an extent as to give them an unnatural
appearance was once popular under the *tako-zukuri*
(lit. octopus-cultivation) method, but this method is
no longer considered correct. Then there is a type of
bonsai in which the trunk of the tree is twisted like a

screw. A group of bonsai fanciers used to think highly of such types. But this kind of bonsai cannot be classed as real bonsai, if fidelity to nature is to be respected in this branch of art. Bonsai lovers of today are generally inclined to think such plants are too unnatural, almost grotesque.

Then we have what is technically called *saba-miki* (lit. split trunk). This is a bonsai in which the greater part of the trunk has decayed, leaving nothing but the core. Such a bonsai suggests an aged tree that has outlived stubborn battles with the elements.

The trunk of a tree suitable for bonsai treatment should taper gradually toward the top. Trunks which have had their tops chopped off to reduce their height are regarded, from an aesthetic point of view, as unsuitable for bonsai treatment.

Lower part of the trunks and roots of aged twin trees

BRANCHES

A large tree growing in the fields and on the hills generally has many branches, each one ramifying into a network of twigs increasing progressively in number toward the tip. It is impossible to make the branches of a bonsai grow in the correct proportion, as to size and number, to match the trunk. Nor should bonsai foliage be so dense as to hide entirely the beauty of the trunk.

The branches must harmonize with the trunk in length and thickness. And the finer the twigs each branch is divided towards the tip, the more valuable is the bonsai.

The branches of an aged tree should have a hoary look even at their tips. The top of any aged tree, if it has been treated properly for years, should also be thickly covered with twigs. One can, in fact, tell whether a bonsai has been well cultivated or not by looking at the tips of its branches.

An interesting arrangement of the branches and flowers of a bonsai

Closely branch-
ed top of a tree

There is a group of expert opinion which declares that in the arrangement or disposition of branches of a bonsai there should be a law as rigid as in the art of *ikebana* or flower arrangement. But in my opinion, bonsai, which should follow the rule of naturalness, should be tied down by no such law, for no law governs trees growing in their natural state.

It has been, and still is today sometimes, the custom for a guest to inspect and admire a bonsai placed as an ornament on the *tokonoma*, or alcove, or standing with a *byobu* (folding screen) for its background. For this reason bonsai were in the past cultivated so that there would be both a right and a wrong side, from which to view them.

But with the exception of a few, most bonsai are now cultivated by a careful pruning of the branches so that they can be appreciated from all sides.

If left severely alone, the branches are liable to devel-op too thick a crown to be in harmony with the trunks.

Nor is that all. Such a crown is liable to make bonsai look altogether too large to be suitable for interior decoration. For this reason trimming or pruning is needed from time to time to keep a bonsai from growing too large. It is almost as foolish not to prune fruit trees bearing large fruit as not to trim the branches in a bonsai. There was a time when the branches were bent into the shape of a series of the letter S arranged in a row, in order to reduce the periphery. But today few bonsai cultivators, if any, resort to such a method.

LEAVES

It would be ideal if the size of the leaves could also be reduced in proportion to the reduced trunk and branches. With the passage of time, it is true, the size of the leaves of a tree can be reduced to a certain extent, but it is an impossibility to make a platanus leaf as small as a maple leaf. This makes it necessary to choose small-leaved trees for bonsai. Even from among plants of the same genus those with smaller leaves are generally chosen for the purpose.

With broad-leaved trees it is practicable to reduce the size of the leaves to some extent by cultivation during the period of active growth from the time the fresh leaves grow till they fall, which is a process repeated year in and year out. The usual practice is to give the plant enough sunlight and expose it to the wind and give it as little moisture as possible. The idea is to stave off superfluous growth. But care must be taken not to carry it too far; for, when overdone, it is liable to

Keyaki (Keaki)

Photographed in winter
Height: 2 feet

Aka-matsu
(Japanese Red pine)

Height: 1 foot 5 inches
Age: 180 years

result in the production of an unhealthy-looking bonsai.

In the case of needle-leaved trees, the shorter the needles, the better. In this respect, for instance, the *ezo-matsu* (Yesso Spruce) is preferred to the ordinary pine. But even the leaves of these trees vary in size according to varieties. Preference is therefore given to those with shorter needles.

Some deciduous bonsai, such as the *keyaki* (Keaki) and the maple, when their leaves have fallen, are admired for the gracefulness of the formation of their twigs more than when they are covered with verdant foliage. For, when their leaves have fallen, the trunks and boughs of these trees are brought into full view, and we can imagine that we see through the needle-like twigs a mass of clouds or two floating in the sky. For this reason deciduous bonsai trees are generally considered more elegant than needle-leaved evergreens which show no seasonal changes.

The deciduous trees of Japan present a different and always pleasing sight in every season. Their luxuriant foliage in summer, and the richly tinted leaves of autumn are renowned. In the spring also they are very lovely to the eye with their branches and twigs covered with sprouting buds in all the light colors of the rainbow—orange, green, red, purple and yellow, and in the winter they display the peculiar charm mentioned above.

Some of the deciduous trees, however, are prized specially for the beauty of their tinted leaves in the autumn. The most popular of these are the *momiji* (Maple), the *nanakamado* (Mountain Ash), the *haze* (Japanese Wax Tree) and the *tsuta* (Ivy).

Among other charming deciduous trees also amenable to bonsai treatment are the *nire* (Japanese Elm), *yama-zakura* (Mountain Cherry), *akashide* (Loose-flower Hornbeam), *keyaki* (Keaki), *nobara* (Japanese Dog Rose) and *konara* (Small Leaved Oak). The Japanese love to arrange a bonsai of the maiden-hair tree or the wax tree with half of the tinted leaves still on and two or three lying on the pot below, suggesting an autumn scene.

In order to enjoy the tinted foliage of the fall season as it is represented in bonsai fully, it is necessary to keep it in the best of health during the summer season by constant watering and by taking care not to spoil it under a hot sun. Unhealthy leaves are apt to fall without turning yellow.

ROOTAGE

Much is made of well-shaped rootage in bonsai. From the base of a bonsai representing a giant we gain a sense of stability. But a trunk looking like a telephone pole sticking out of the ground fails to give a sense of solidity and stability. The bonsai root which ramifies from the base of the trunk——now above and now under the soil——reminds us of the crawling roots of an age-old tree in the recesses of a mountain, with moss growing on the network of its exposed ramifications. To produce a likeness of such a root in a pot is to enhance the intrinsic value of a bonsai. The bonsai phrase "*ichi-miki, ni-eda, san-nebari*" (lit. First, trunk; secondly, branches; and thirdly, rootage.) is synonymous with the balanced development of a large tree. A bonsai with defective rootage is a failure.

Ideal rootage is usually found in a tree nurtured from a seedling in a pot. The roots of a tree cultivated from a cutting naturally lacks strength to support its trunk. But continued growth in a tray will gradually remedy this defect.

Most of the trees collected from rugged hillsides have poor rootage. But the roots of even such trees may be improved by judicious treatment in the process of transplantation. What is known as *kata-nebari* (one-sided rootage) is not amenable to such treatment. The lack of stability of this form of rootage is overcome by placing a stone at the base of the tree or by planting grass over it. But this makeshift——for makeshift it is——is not considered the best course to take.

In transplanting a bonsai care is taken to arrange its

Roots of an age-old tree

root in waves, in such a way that it is exposed in parts above the soil. As the root is tender and easy to bend, it is not so difficult to manipulate as the branches.

Mayumi
(Japanese Strawberry-Bush)

Nashi (Sand Pear)

Above left: Yamafuji (Japanese Wistaria)
Above right: Kaido (Kaido Crab-Apple)
Below left: Umemodoki (Ilex serrata var. Sieboldii)
Below right: Akashide (Loose-flower Hornbeam)

FLOWERING PLANTS AND
FRUIT TREES

Whether in or out of the flowering season, a bonsai loses much of its value if it is not shapely. It is of primary importance that a bonsai be of elegant proportions.

Chief among the flowering plants suitable for bonsai are the cherry, *rengyo* (Golden Bells), *sazanka* (Sasanqua), *kaido* (Kaido Crab-Apple), *tsutsuji* (Azalea), *nashi* (Sand Pear), *ringo* (Apple), *momo* (Peach), *boke* (Japanese Quince), *sanzashi* (Chinese Hawthorn), *oto* (Cherry), *fuji* (Japanese Wistaria), *obai* (Winter Jasmine), *tsubaki* (Garden Camellia), and *zakuro* (Pomegranate). Of these, the *kaido, nashi, ringo, boke, rengyo, momo, oto,* and *sanzashi* are appreciated for their fruit, as well as for their blossoms, while the *fuji, obai,* and *tsubaki* are cultivated for their flowers only. *Mikan* (Orange tree), *kaki* (Japanese Persimmon), *umemodoki* (Ilex serrata var. Sieboldii), and *mayumi* (Japanese Strawberry-Bush) are cultivated as bonsai because of their fruit.

Large flowers are out of place with dwarf trees. A magnolia bonsai in bloom is more like a twig bearing flowers, stuck into a pot. The camellia flower is also regarded as too large to suit bonsai taste, and bonsai cultivators have succeeded in evolving a species of this plant with flowers no bigger than the finger-tips.

Bonsai flowers are appreciated not so much for their rich colors as for their elegance. And a delicate scent is preferred to a more powerful one. Take for example the *ume* (Japanese Apricot*). Among the 300 odd species that exist, pride of place is given to the one that puts forth snow-white flowers of fine shape. Bonsai cultivators seek refined elegance in flowers. For this reason field flowers are often used for bonsai, because of their rich rustic beauty. Among the wild flowers so treated are the *miyama-kaido* (Kaido Crab-Apple), the mountain cherry, the *mansaku* (Japanese Witch Hazel), the *tsutsuji* (Azalea), the *nobara* (Japanese Dog Rose) and the *nindo* (Japanese Honeysuckle).

What has been said about bonsai flowers can also be said of the fruit-bearing bonsai trees. Trees with large fruit are not suitable for bonsai. It is possible to make such trees as the *kaki* (Japanese Persimmon), *nashi* (Sand Pear), and *ringo* (Apple) bear fruit so large that their total volume will surpass that of the earth contained in the pot. But this horticultural technique is not admired in the art of bonsai. Bonsai experts think highly of a wild persimmon bonsai with fruit that harmonizes with the tree in size.

Other wild trees congenial to bonsai treatment by reason of their pretty, small-sized fruit include the *umemodoki* (Ilex serrata var. Sieboldii), *mayumi* (Japanese

---

* Although in various books on Japan, including guide books, the *ume* is usually referred to as the *plum,* in this brochure we have adopted the term *Japanese apricot* at the suggestion of Dr. Hisayoshi Takeda.

Above: Tsubaki (Garden Camellia)

Below: Ume (Japanese Apricot)

Nashi (Sand Pear)

Kaki (Japanese Persimmon)

Strawberry-Bush), *tsuru-umemodoki* (Celastrus articulatus), *haze* (Japanese Wax Tree), *nanakamado* (Mountain Ash), *uguisu-kagura* (Lonicera gracilipes), *Yamaboshi* (Japanese Dogwood or Kousa), *gamazumi* (Viburnum dilatatum), *kuko* (Box-thorn), *nishikigi* (Winged Spindle-Tree) and *mamegaki* (Date Plum). The idea behind the training of these wild trees for bonsai is so that we can admire the fruit hanging from their tiny branches like so many pieces of coral and amber, or pearls or other gems, and appreciate them without taking the trouble of wending our way right to their natural homes.

Kaki (Japanese Persimmon)

[SHI-TSUKI] OR USE OF STONES
FOR EFFECT

What is technically styled *ishi-tsuki* is a form of bon-sai arrangement. This method of using rough stones for effect—for such is the meaning of this technical term—is resorted to in representing ancient trees perch-ed on mountain crags or overhanging beach cliffs against which the waves wash, or valley precipices beneath which mountain streams spurt. In the realistic effect it gives to the scene suggested, this method is like that used in *bonkei* (tray-landscape). But *ishi-tsuki* differs from *bonkei*, because in the former we can enjoy the seasonal changes in the appearance of the trees and watch its growth.

In the *ishi-tsuki* type one has no small difficulty in finding the right stone for the right tree, so that together they may suggest a landscape. Suppose you succeed in stumbling on just the right stone to match. You still need a great deal of experience and skill in planting the tree *on* that stone to advantage.

There are two ways of producing *ishi-tsuki* effect. One is to arrange the root of the tree in such a way that it will embrace the stone, with its fibrous tips anchored in the soil of the tray. The other way is to fill the cav-ity or depression in the stone with soil and plant the tree there. In the first method the root of the tree must be

Above: Ezo-matsu (Yesso Spruce) cultivated on a stone
Below: A closer view of the same

Above : Tokaede (Trident Maple)

Below : Ezo-matsu (Yesso Spruce)

Left: Goyo-
matsu (Five-
needled Pine)

Below: Goyo-
matsu and a
creeper

long and strong.

On the other hand the root of the tree to be used in the latter method has to be short, with plenty of ramifications. Care must be taken that one of the roots reaches the bottom of the stone which, for this purpose, stands in the basin which contains water instead of earth. As the tips of the root are thus soaked in water, the tree will keep alive without frequent watering.

The soil used for filling the depression of such a stone is a peat-like variety, produced when reeds are buried in the ground. The use of this kind of soil keeps the bonsai alive for a long time without frequent transplantation.

Among common trees amenable to this *ishi-tsuki* treatment are the *goyo-matsu* (Five-needled Pine), *ezo-matsu* (Yesso Spruce), *kaede* (Maple-tree), and *shimpa-ku* (Chinese Juniper). The maple-tree cultivated thus usually develops in time a root flattened like a plate, which eventually clasps the stone entirely.

As has already been stated, the object of *ishi-tsuki* is to suggest a bit of gorge scenery or seascape. Hence the use of a tray filled with water, and not with soil. This type of bonsai is particularly popular in the summer. Moss-covered stones used for the purpose go well with the trees, thereby adding charm to the scenery so suggested.

BABY BONSAI

It may be because the extreme always has an attraction for many people that the Japanese have succeeded in reducing the scale of bonsai to a size even smaller than the usual bonsai, creating what is called *mame-bonsai* or baby bonsai.

An ordinary bonsai is usually about two feet high and two feet broad. This is regarded as a convenient size for both enjoyment and handling. Anything under one foot in height is called a *katate-mochi bonsai;* that

Omi-kaido (Malus prunifolia—A Crab Apple) — A specimen of baby bonsai

is, a bonsai capable of being carried in one hand. A bonsai of this size is often seen as an ornament on a desk. A smaller one is nicknamed "baby." Often only about two inches and half in height, this kind of midget bonsai can be placed on the palm of the hand—two or three at once. And there are smaller ones still. So tiny indeed is this pigmy of pigmies, dubbed

A five-year old
Goyo-matsu
(Five - needled
Pine) grown
from a seed

"*shito-bonsai*" (lit. finger-tip), that it can be put on the tip of a finger, as its name indicates. The pot used for this Lilliputian bonsai is no bigger than the size of a chestnut. The most remarkable thing about it is that such trees as the five-needled pine, *keyaki* (Keaki) and *shimpaku* (Chinese Juniper), trees which as a rule grow to be very large, are capable of being treated as "finger-tip" bonsai—and often last scores of years at that. Such an achievement suggests something created by a magician with a flourish of his wand. Here again we find substantiation for the remark of a foreign critic who credits the Japanese with a genius for small things.

In making baby bonsai, the materials to work on are usually picked out from among the seedlings growing in the leaf-mould or in washed-out soil found on the tiled roof of an ancient mausoleum or in a fissure in a rock,—seedlings which, though age-old, are so stunted by nature that they show no visible signs of development.

A shelf for the display of baby bonsai

Sometimes ordinary seedlings or cuttings are used, but they are greatly inferior to those chosen from among natural specimens.

The late Mr. Yorinaga Matsudaira, sometime Speaker of the House of Peers, was a rare collector of baby bonsai. He had something like one thousand specimens of

Hinoki
(Hinoki Cypress)

Height : 3 inches
Age : 6 years

excellent quality, which he himself tended with great enthusiasm. It seems a pity that Japan today has no collector of unusual bonsai worthy to be called his successor.

It may be added that baby bonsai, like their bigger cousins, perform their botanical functions in season to admiration; they bear blossoms and fruit like Aaron's rod.

Another specimen of baby bonsai
—Ume (Japanese Apricot)

Omi-kaido (Malus prunifolia —A Crab-Apple)

Kaki (Japanese persimmon)

SANSUI-SEKI OR KEI-SEKI

The search of beauty in natural stones is the result of an effort to attain the ideal in nature. Such beauty is found in moist, moss-covered stones which are often found in deep gorges or in the inmost recesses of mountains, and which give an impression of being pregnant with eternal mystery.

Japan is a volcanic country, abounding in stones of every shape and description. Perhaps because of the very abundance of beautiful stones and their variety, the love of stones is inborn in the people. To men of good taste and discrimination a stone has character and individuality, which can be appreciated only when they can display it in the proper place and setting.

A stone is to a bonsai what a piano accompanist is to a violin player. Stones are often used to add to the effect of a bonsai. Reference has already been made to the practice of using stones for this purpose. But that is not all there is to the use of stones for scenic effects. Sometimes a stone is placed by itself, and proves as effective as the whole bonsai. Such stones are called *sui-seki* (water-stones) or *sansui-seki* (landscape-stones) and are given a prominent place among bonsai.

Mountain streams in Japan are a depository of stones of all sizes and shapes. It is there that the Japanese seek for landscape-stones. Of these the following varieties

Toyamakei-seki (Distant mountain stone)

are the most important:

Toyamakei-seki (lit. Distant mountain stone). This kind of stone is intended to suggest a distant view of mountains rising one above another, or of a chain of mountains looming on the horizon.

Iwagata-ishi (lit. Seashore stone). This stone gives a suggestion of crags towering above the seashore or the lakeshore; it is designed to conjure up in the imagination the kind of rocks that waves break against or those that rise from the limpid waters of a lake.

Taki-ishi (lit. Cascade stone). This name is given to the sort of stone which has a depression in it suggestive of a gorge. When streaked with white, such a depression is supposed to suggest a waterfall.

Tokei-seki (lit. Island scenery stone). The function of this stone is to suggest an island rising out from the sea or floating on the emerald waters of a lake.

Kayaya-ishi (Kuzuya-ishi) (lit. Thatched roof stone). This is so called because it is shaped not un-

Iwagata-ishi (Seashore stone)

like the thatched roofs so characteristic of rural Japan. Hence, such a stone is used in suggesting a country scene.

Mizutamari-ishi (lit. Water pool stone). So called from the fact that this kind of stone has a cavity which, when filled with water, suggests a mountain lake or a pool in a stream.

All these stones, except the "thatched roof stone," are generally placed in trays containing water. But sometimes, as in the case of the "distant mountain stone," they are put in shallow trays, surrounded with earth and covered with moss, or arranged in such a way as to suggest a wilderness by means of field grasses planted around.

What is more important, such stones are picked out from among rare specimens of the handiworks of Nature, despite the fact that artificial examples can be more realistic in their effect. They are more suggestive than realistic; productive of aesthetic sentiments in fancy and imagination. Appreciation of landscape stones should

Tokei-seki (Island scenery stone)

transcend theory. This may sound somewhat esoteric, but there is poetry in a true appreciation of landscape stones.

Ezo-mats (Yesso Spruce) cultivated on a stone

HERBS AS BONSAI

Fields carpeted with brown withering herbs remind us that spring cannot be far behind; that the grasses are getting ready for their winter slumber, only to wake and sprout again with the advance of spring. In herbs, as well as in arbors we find charms born of seasonal changes. Naturally enough, such herbs lend themselves to bonsai treatment. Chief among such plants are the *sasa* (Dwarf Bamboo), the *sekisho* (Grass Sweet Flag), the *ashi* (Common Reed), the *susuki* (Miscanthus sinensis), the *shida* (fern) and the *iwahiba* (Resurrection Plant). The first-named is generally considered to be of paramount importance among them. These plants show sufficient

Bonsai of wild flowers

seasonal changes to give enjoyment to the man of taste, as well as to the man of science. Unlike these popular plants which are found abundantly in the fields and mountains, garden flowers do not appeal to the man of bonsai taste, let alone those hot-house herbs which are nurtured so as to flower out of season. This is because they fail to make him feel that naturalness which comes from the changes of the four seasons.

The common run of urban people so inured to the din, dust and bustle of life are aware of the seasonal changes only through the calendar, if not through changes in the climate. To such people even a pot of bonsai grass may excite their aesthetic feeling, if they have a modicum of such feeling. Midget trees representing giant arbors or luxuriant woods are not the only things adapted to bonsai treatment. Even field grasses may be treated as bonsai; for, after all, appreciation of the beautiful is within the mind of the person who looks at it. When treated with the masterly skill of an expert bonsai maker, even the grasses planted in clusters are as valuable as the excellent examples of age-old bonsai representing giant trees, at least in the eyes of one who has a flair for things of beauty.

Spring wild flowers

Autumn wild flowers

CULTIVATION

Bonsai culture is the art of growing trees or grasses in trays containing no more soil than is absolutely necessary on the basis of a close observation of their development in a natural state. It is an art that demands not only scientific observation but also care born of motherly affection. Who loves Nature is richly rewarded by Nature. It is surprising how a bonsai can live for centuries and gratify man's love of Nature by showing its characteristic features according to the season. Only one who nurses bonsai by pruning and watering them faithfully can fully appreciate the pleasure derivable from the change of seasons.

As has been pointed out above, the bonsai needs to be tended with the affection which a mother shows for her child. Water your bonsai immediately when you come home after a hot summer day's work, and you will feel as pleased as a man who makes his wife and children happy by giving them what they want. It is not too much to say that a bonsai proves of the greatest interest only to those who take care of it, watering can in hand. One may regard it as little short of a miracle that a pigmy tree, a miniature copy of a towering giant, can be kept alive literally for several hundred years in a small tray-like pot, but it is an achievement technically feasible with judicious care in cultivation. An example will

Shimpaku (Chinese Juniper)

Aka-matsu
(Japanese Red Pine)

Height 1 ft. 8 in
150 years old

suffice. A *goyo-no-matsu* (Five-needled Pine) which was a pet bonsai of Iemitsu, third Tokugawa Shogun (1584—1651), passed subsequently into the hands of an emperor and is still alive today in the palace in all its beauty.

This is due to various devices and methods applied in accordance with plant physiology; to religious care and untiring effort. The price of neglecting to water your bonsai in midsummer even for a day will have to be paid in a withered plant. You might as well plough the field and forget the seed as commit such negligence.

The fundamental object of bonsai cultivation is to express natural beauty, charm or sublimity as best you can. The ultimate object of a potted plant is to make it send forth rich flowers; that of a potted vegetable is to make it bear big fruit. In a bonsai what is respected more than anything else is the poetical feeling it evokes. For this reason manuring and watering, if done haphazardly, will not help attain the real object of bonsai culture. Excessive growth has to be checked to a proper extent. A bonsai, however old and rare, would be judged of little worth, if it were devoid of magnetic charm. Of this fact veteran bonsai cultivators are aware as they strive to create their masterpieces.

There are roughly seven factors in successful bonsai cultivation. They are: (1) soil, (2) transplantation, (3) watering, (4) care in placing the pots in summer and winter, (5) the nipping of buds or pruning, (6) manuring and (7) extermination of harmful insects and the prevention of diseases.

Ezo-matsu
(Yesso Spruce)

Height: 1 ft. 5 in.

SOIL

As has already been stated, the important thing in bonsai cultivation is to bring out the greatest effect with the use of the least amount of soil. From olden times different soils have been used in different districts. But the principle is the same; that is to say, it consists in selecting the soil most capable of preserving moisture and of admitting air. The best kind of soil now being used in Japan is a hard soil which generally forms a stratum beneath the cultivated soil of the land. When weathered, this type of soil becomes powdered. The usual practice is to pulverize hard soil that has not yet weathered, sift it to remove both powdered soil and clod, and pick out only such soil as is granular in form and of the uniform size of about one millimeter. The soil thus obtained is then mixed with a proper amount of sandy tuff. The amount of sandy soil to be used varies with the trees. Generally speaking, more than 50% of this sandy soil is used for evergreens and 20% for flowering plants and broad-leaved trees. For the latter something like 10% of a soil formed of decayed leaves (the sort of soil made from fallen leaves heaped up and left decaying for more than a year) is further added.

The reason why granular soil of a uniform size is used is that it not only admits air better than other forms of soil, but the spaces in the soil also are capable of retaining

Ringo (Apple)

moisture like holes in a sponge. This requires less frequent watering than otherwise. And there are other advantages. Once the soil is saturated with moisture, the air in the spaces is pushed out. Then, the moisture becomes gradually absorbed by the root-hairs or evaporates into the sunshine or wind, and is again replaced by air. This cycle is repeated, and while the old moisture is replaced by the new, the air and moisture are continually interchanging to fill the spaces in the soil. Now soft granular soil itself retains moisture, a fact which prevents the root-hairs from becoming dried, even when the spaces in the soil are completely devoid of moisture, until the next watering of the plant. Another thing to remember is that soil with grains of sand that are angular is better than that with round grains. For angular sand is more effective in stimulating the branching action of fibrous roots and enables the root to permeate the entire portion of the soil in the pot. Bonsai cultivators have proved this fact through long experience. The root of a plant tends to expand outward radially. Now within the narrow scope of a pot this propensity is greatly restricted. The walls of a pot cause the roots to go round and round beside them, eventually weakening the roots greatly. Here the presence of angular sand in the pot becomes useful. When a fibrous root strikes against such sand, it cannot but alter its course. This deviation from its regular course stimulates a branching of the root-hairs, thereby causing the roots to fill the soil of the pot gradually.

In the absence of soft sand (the sort of sand which

is so cracked that it will break when beaten lightly), either a granular form of weathered volcanic ash or pulverized limestone will work, if mixed with soil. This mixture of sand and soil has the effect of preventing the soil from hardening. Sometimes the substitution of the husks of cotton-seeds for sand does the job, not so much for evergreens as for broad-leaved deciduous trees.

When a great deal of moisture is desired, charcoal pulverized into a uniform size is used instead. But this must be used in moderation, for charcoal is liable to absorb manure too freely, thereby promoting an undesirable growth of the bonsai. For this reason it is not advisable to use charcoal for certain kinds of vegetation. A little of it can, of course, be used with profit to the plant.

TRANSPLANTATION

The roots of trees in their natural state usually radiate unrestricted in all directions. But they cannot do that in the limited space of a tray-pot. Yet, strangely enough, a bonsai can and does live to a great age, and in a healthy condition at that. It stands to reason that the soil confined within a small pot will lose its nourishing power in a short time. The three nourishing elements prerequisite to plant life—phosphoric acid, potassium and nitrogen—can be replenished, it is true, by means of fertilizers, but the plant requires other elements such as lime, sulphur, magnesium and iron as well, though in very small quantities. These may be found in the soil, but are soon exhausted in the small space of the pot. So if left untended for some length of time, the bonsai suffers malnutrition and will consequently wither sooner or later. The system of water cultivation which is in general use in America may solve the problem of supplying the deficiency of such elements. But it may not be so easy to figure out the exact amount required for each individual bonsai, each of which has characteristics peculiarly its own. Here is where the need for transplantation comes in. The chief object of the process is to refresh the soil of the pot.

Another object is to rearrange the ramifications of the roots of the bonsai to be transplanted. When left in the pot too long, the bonsai will become root-bound, that is, the roots will eventually develop into a mass of hairs which prevent the absorption of fertilizers. If left longer, the volume of the roots will increase, lifting the soil surface above the rim of the pot. Hence the necessity of pruning the roots, removing all the old parts no longer capable of activity and supplying new soil to stimulate the growth of new root-hairs.

Different bonsai require different intervals for transplantation. Some are suited for spring transplantation and others for autumn. Generally speaking, evergreens are transplanted once every four or five years. (In the case of the *sugi* or Japanese cedar*, once in two years.) Flowering plants and fruit trees must be transplanted once every year; and broad-leaved deciduous trees, such as the *kaede* (Maple) and the Japanese elm, once every two years.

The seasons for transplantation vary with the regional climates. But a close observation of the condition of each plant should dictate the time it should be transplanted. This means that different bonsai should be transplanted at different times. Generally speaking the best time for transplantation is just when the plant awakes from its winter inactivity, or, in other words, when its buds are beginning to swell.

There are exceptions to the rule. For example, the

---

* Although in various books on Japan, including guide books, the *sugi* is usually referred to as the *cryptomeria*, in this brochure we have adopted the term *Japanese cedar* at the suggestion of Dr. Hisayoshi Takeda.

Nire (Japanese Elm)

Boke (Japanese Quince)　　　　　　*Height: 2 feet*

84～

boke (Japanese Quince) and the *obai* (Winter Jasmine) which heralds the coming of spring up on the highlands when everything is still in the grip of winter, are generally transplanted just as they are beginning to shed their leaves, probably because they continue their growth right through the winter.

In Japan citrus trees and other evergreens are transplanted, as a rule, when the temperature is from 60° F. to 70° F., or in other words toward the end of April, while the azalea is best transplanted after its blooming season is over.

Though spring is the best time for transplantation, bonsai can also be transplanted in autumn, but as much before midautumn as possible. Early winter is a little too late, because of the frost. What is important is to allow enough time for the growth of fresh root-hairs before the plant becomes dormant after transplantation. Autumn transplantation is impossible for subtropical plants.

METHODS OF TRANSPLANTATION

All bonsai pots have drain-holes in the bottom; the smaller ones have one and the larger ones three or five each. These apertures are designed to drain off the excess water and at the same time to admit air into the soil. These drain-holes are technically called "eyes." The eye or eyes of a bonsai pot must not be "closed" or clogged. If left "wide open," however, the soil will leak out of them. This has led to the device of lids or covers. The simplest forms of "lid" is made of fragments of a pot. But this hardly does duty for a good drain-hole or ventilator. The most ideal "eye lid" is a little unglazed earthenware vessel shaped like a Japanese tea cup, and having innumerable small holes all over it. This cup-like affair is put on the "eye," bottom up. The only drawback of this cover is that it displaces a certain amount of soil in the pot. A contraption like a cross section of a lotus root honeycombed with holes has recently been devised. A simpler yet quite effective cover is made of wire netting with a fine mesh.

The "eye" or "eyes" properly screened, the bottom of the pot is now covered with two or three layers of hard clods about the size of a soy-bean or a hemp seed. If such clods are not available, pieces of charcoal or crushed stone of about the same size will answer the purpose. Above these layers of clods is placed another

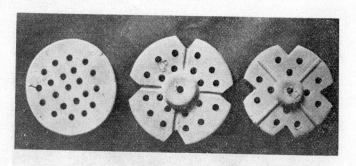

Unglazed earthenware "eye-lids"

layer of clod (or charcoal or stone pieces) of a little
smaller size, the object being to prevent the soil from
falling through the spaces formed between the clods.

These preparations made, the business of adjusting
the root is then commenced. The lower part of a pot-
bound bonsai when pulled out of the pot is a mass of
roots. The first thing to do is to break the lump gently
and slowly with a pointed stick, taking care not to break
off the root-hairs. About two-thirds of the old soil
should be removed this way. In the case of flowering
plants and fruit trees, the old soil may removed entirely
from the bonsai.

The extent of root-pruning differs according to the
different bonsai. The young plants are root-pruned
freely and the old only slightly. In the case of the latter,
only the root-tips of little vitality are cut off, care being
taken that the new fibrous roots are left intact. The foliage of a plant grows in proportion to the quantity
of its roots. In order to produce many leafy branches,

Root-pruning

it is necessary for the plant to have plenty of fibrous roots. A plant with a few rough branches presupposes a few, long, thick roots radiating through the soil. So the important thing is to root-prune a bonsai judiciously at the time of transplantation. Herein lies the secret of keeping bonsai alive for ages.

The root-pruning operation must be carried out speedily in a damp room, well sheltered from both sun and wind. Care must be taken not to expose the roots to the sun and wind.

When properly root-pruned, the bonsai is put back in the pot, all ready for replantation. Meticulous care must be taken to place the plant at the right depth and in the right position in the pot. The next step is to fill the pot with soil. The extent of pressure put on the root also varies with the trees. With evergreens, especially with pine trees, it is the custom to press the soil hard, but in the case of broad-leaved deciduous trees, the soil need not be pressed so hard. The important thing is, however, to see that the soil gets well into every portion of the pot, filling every possible space at a uniform hardness, so as to allow water sprinkled over it to permeate every part uniformly.

The loam used in replanting bonsai has to be quite dry; it is easier, however, to handle this kind of soil if it is moistened a bit by a fine spray of water, prior to the planting. If the soil is moistened too much, it may become too hard through its own weight for the water to drain off properly.

If a planted tree shows any signs of unsteadiness, the important thing is to keep it steady by fastening strings or wires from the trunk out in all directions.

The next thing to do is to water the plant. If you should pour water over the soil before it is firmly settled, the surface layer is liable to be washed away. It is therefore advisable to sprinkle water gently with a watering-can or a spray with a finely perforated nozzle. This sprinkling is kept up till the water comes oozing out of the drain-hole or holes.

After the replanting is over, the bonsai must be sheltered carefully from both sun and wind; it is not safe to take it out into the air until the roots have started activity again.

Yuzu (Citrus Junos)

WHERE TO PLACE BONSAI

Exposure to the elements, to sunshine, rain, dew, etc. is indispensable to the growth of trees and plants in their natural state. But bonsai are liable to be denied this pre-requisite because of their being so handy to carry that they can be placed in any place, as, for example, indoors, under the eaves, etc.

It may be superfluous to state why exposure to the elements is so necessary to plant life. You may think such a thing as wind will do more harm than good. Too strong a wind does harm, it is true, to plants, but a light, fresh wind is useful as it renders them strong and resistant to diseases. Trees cultivated in an urban area are often lacking in vigor, due partly to the scarcity of night dew.

Insufficient exposure to the sun weakens the foliage of a plant, reducing the sap, and makes it like one nur-tured in a glass-house. Take such a weakly plant out under a hot sun, all of a sudden, and you will find it will wither in a short time.

Different species of plants react differently upon ex-posure to the summer sun. The pine, the *ume* (Japanese Apricot) and the pomegranate for example, can stand the burning sun of midsummer all day long, whereas alpine plants prefer the shade.

Trees whose habitat was in the recesses of mountains

will find it an ordeal to be exposed to the sun throughout the day in flat country. Such exposure will gradually lead to an untimely shedding of leaves.

When a bonsai is kept out in the broiling summer sun, the side of the pot nearest the sun will get exceedingly hot. Naturally the roots of a tree inured to the climate of the high mountains will be injured if the soil reaches a temperature of 40°C. or more. This makes it necessary to provide some sort of shelter for the plant or keep it from the summer sunshine. It is customary for a bonsai cultivator to shelter his plants with a reed-screen put up about seven feet above the shelves on which they are arranged. Such a screen is not necessary if one has only a few bonsai. All that is needed in such a case is to put something between them and the strong afternoon sun from the west. It is after two in the afternoon that the sun is the strongest, so the thing to remember is to give the bonsai as much sunshine as possible in the morning and very little in the afternoon. But it is not wise to keep bonsai altogether under the eaves or in the shade of trees, because of the fact that underbrush often has a sick and weakly appearance.

Both in spring and autumn enough sunshine should be given to all bonsai throughout the day, especially from the sprouting season to the end of May when the new leaves reach their full development. Lack of sunshine will encourage the growth of a sickly type of foliage,—large, flimsy leaves too weak to stand the powerful sun of the summer even for a moment.

In the cold season different species of bonsai require

In winter bonsai are usually kept on shelves screened on three sides and above so as to keep the plants from rain and wind

different degrees of protection according to the climate and temperature. The pine-tree, the *todo-matsu* (Sakhalin Fir), the *ezo-matsu* (Yesso Spruce), and the *shimpaku* (Chinese Juniper), for example, are little affected by rain or snow, but broad-leaved deciduous plants have to be kept in a warm place or in a spot protected from the cold weather. The treatment given a bonsai during the summer determines whether it will be able to pass the winter season in good condition or not.

As for the plants growing in the temperate zone, the hardy ones may be kept out-of-doors safely, but some sort of protection against the snow is expedient, if not absolutely necessary, lest their branches break under the weight of the snow. Such protection is also useful when there is any fear that the pot may break because of expanding ice. A bamboo or reed screen put up over the bonsai in such a way as to shelter them from the north wind will serve as a protection of this kind.

Except for those intended for quick blooming, bonsai must never be kept in a glass-house. They must lie quiescent during the winter, and revive with the coming of spring. If the plants are placed suddenly and unexpectedly in an atmosphere of high temperature in the winter time, they will send forth buds out of season,— but these buds will be weak and sickly.

The same is true of fruit-bearing bonsai, such as the pear, the peach, the Japanese apricot and the persimmon. It is essential that such bonsai be kept in a place maintained at low temperature, ranging from zero to five degrees centigrade during the winter, care being taken to prevent the soil in the pot from freezing. However, if the soil freezes at night, and melts the following day, not much harm is done.

With regard to such plants as the pomegranate and the azalea, which dislike cold weather, they must, of course, be protected against soil frost. But as most plants can bear the cold to some degree, it is necessary to study to what extent each individual plant is susceptible to the cold.

What the bonsai fancier fears more than anything else in winter is damage, not so much from cold, as from dryness. Winter is the dry season in Japan, and the soil in the limited space of a bonsai pot is liable to get dry,

Ezo-matsu
(Yesso Spruce)

Height: 1 ft. 8 in.

Yamazakura
(Mountain Cherry)

Height: 1 ft. 5 in.

when the foliage of the tree is exposed to a cold wind, a condition very damaging to bonsai. The important thing is therefore to keep your bonsai in not too dry a place and to see that the soil retains about 40% of the moisture passing through it. For if the soil retains all the water it is capable of holding in the space of the pot, it will become one mass of ice should the water freeze. Such a danger may be warded off by providing for air spaces in the soil.

WATERING

In spite of the best of care in every other way a bonsai will wither if not watered. A bonsai should be sprinkled with water whenever the soil gets dry. On the other hand, to water a bonsai when the soil is not dry is as harmful as to neglect watering it when the soil is thoroughly dry. One should give up the idea of cultivating bonsai if one thinks it troublesome to water the plant whenever necessary.

It is not necessary to water your bonsai constantly. Just water it at regular intervals, however hot the sun may be. Recent methods of bonsai cultivation are rational; even the amount of water to be retained in the pot being adjusted, as was stated in a previous chapter, by properly preparing and mixing various types of soil at the time of transplantation.

As was pointed out previously, the soil used in bonsai cultivation is granular and the clods are as porous and permeable to moisture as a sponge, so to speak,—or something like the fine meshes of a net covered with watery membranes, when just dipped in water. Once water sprinkled on the soil in the pot remains there after saturation, then it is not necessary to use a watering-can more than twice a day—once in the morning and once before sunset—even in midsummer. In this connection I can give a good method to make the water re-

Yanagi (Weeping Willow) cultivated on a stone

main in the pot after saturation. It is like this: first sprinkle water gently with a watering-can till it begins to flow out of the drain hole, and then after a minute or so start sprinkling again till the water begins to drain away for the second time. This shows that the soil has now become thoroughly saturated with water. This way of supplying water is necessary only in summertime. In spring and autumn all that is needed is to sprinkle water over the soil whenever it shows signs of drying.

From spring right on to early summer all plants pass through a period of vigorous growth. During this time bonsai should not be watered overmuch. For, one important rule in bonsai cultivation is to check overgrowth, and excessive moisture during this period is liable to stimulate an overgrowth of foliage, to the detriment of the outward appearance of the plant. So it is considered a good thing to refrain from watering bonsai even to the extent of letting the tips of the shoots wither a bit. This is particularly the case with fruit and flower-bearing trees; for an excessive supply of water during this period of growth makes them too full of sap to put forth flower buds. Veteran bonsai fanciers are therefore very careful in watering bonsai.

In addition to sprinkling water on bonsai soil, it is sometimes necessary to water the foliage of a bonsai with a sprinkler or a spray. In places where the dew falls at night, this is not so important, but in urban areas this sprinkling is found very useful because both foliage and branches are liable to be covered with dust and soot, which is very bad for the plant. The bad effects of soot on foliage are especially discernible in such trees as the Japanese red pine and the *sugi* (Japanese Cedar). Hence, the necessity of cleaning the bonsai leaves from time to time. But "leaf-spray" must not be given in broad daylight; it is usually more effective before sunset than if done in the morning. The Japanese seem to enjoy the coolness of summer evenings more by looking at the bonsai leaves sparkling with drops of sprinkled water.

Fuji (Japanese Wistaria)

Sugi (Japanese Cedar)   *Height: 1 ft. 8 in.*

FERTILIZERS

There is no need to say that fertilizers are very important in bonsai culture, since a bonsai plant of the maximum dimensions permissible by the dictates of beauty must needs live in the minimum amount of soil. It is true that no bonsai will die even if not manured for a twelvemonth or so, but if this life of austerity continues longer it will gradually weaken and wither away. A bonsai is not dead wood, nor is it a stone. It is alive, and being alive, it will respond to affectionate treatment by healthy growth.

A novice is usually uncertain when, how often and to what extent he should manure the soil of a bonsai plant. As all bonsai can go without fertilizers for a year or so, too much manuring is liable to hurt rather than help it: in fact one should manure bonsai in moderation. The Japanese adage says: "There are mothers who make the fatal error of killing their babies through overfeeding, but there are none who kill their babies by underfeeding." The same may be said of bonsai culture. When manured too much the growth of bonsai will be affected adversely and the plant will eventually become sickly and grotesque in form.

The three elements of a good plant fertilizer—phosphoric acid, potassium and nitrogen—should be given in judicious proportions. Scientific attempts have been made to determine standards by which to measure the amount of each element that is necessary in proportion to the volume of the soil, but no satisfactory results have so far been obtained. This is because the need for these elements varies with the kind of tree, its age and the density of its foliage. In the cultivation of chrysanthemums and other flowers, which are generally grown in pots of uniform size and shape, it is fairly easy to determine such standards. But it is not so easy in case of plants which demand more particular treatment.

It is said that many of the bonsai which were shipped abroad showed, a year or two later, a growth as vigorous as saplings in a natural state, losing their elegant appearance and all value as bonsai. In all probability this was due to inordinate manuring and watering. As has already been said more than once, the bonsai is a symbol of a life of austerity. Confined as it is, within the narrow scope of a pot it must show a balanced growth of trunk, branches and leaves in order to be of aesthetic value. Therefore, manure bonsai in moderation, if you wish to have a model plant.

Now regarding the kinds of fertilizer best suited for bonsai, I would recommend an animal or vegetable manure of slow effect in preference to chemical fertilizers. Such old standbys as oil cake, powdered bone, and wood ash are, for example, considered efficacious. When oil cake is used, it is necessary to let it putrefy thoroughly in water and then to use the solution so prepared. For all bonsai except the coniferae, fruit trees and flowering trees, this solution alone is sufficient. Fruit trees such

Sanzashi
(Chinese Hawthorn)

Height: 1 ft. 6 in.

Mikan (Orange Tree)

as the Japanese persimmon, the sand pear, the apple, the grape vine and the citrus tree require a large amount of manure with a phosphoric acid content; in the fruit-bearing season, particularly, a small amount of a solution containing the three aforesaid elements must be applied daily or on alternate days. The use of such a solution generally works wonders.

Needle-leaved trees which are transplanted in spring need not be manured till late summer, but must be fertilized in autumn. All the nourishment contained in the loam used at the time of transplanting will have been absorbed by autumn. This makes it necessary to manure such bonsai twice or three times from about the autumn equinox to the middle of November to give them sufficient nutrition and enable them to pass the winter in good health, ready to sprout again in the spring.

PRUNING

Even as fruit trees need pruning, so bonsai have to be trimmed if they are to remain in perfect form. Different bonsai are pruned in different seasons. Insofar as pruning is concerned, bonsai may be divided into two categories—(1) fruit- and flower-bearing trees and (2) others. As in orchards, all overgrown parts of fruit-tree bonsai must be lopped off. Flowering plants, such as the *ume* (Japanese Apricot) and the cherry-tree, put forth flower-buds from twigs of the previous year, so the practice is to prune off young twigs near the base, leaving two buds behind, after the blossoms are gone. Other bonsai must be nipped literally in the bud to check overgrowth.

The pine-tree and other trees of its kind first put forth shoots at the tips of their branches, from which later on needles will sprout. To check their overgrowth and stimulate branching, the usual practice is to pinch off the longer ones with the finger tips leaving a bit behind at the base. The shorter ones are left untrimmed. In the case of the *tohi* (Hondo Spruce), the *todo-matsu* (Sakhalin Fir), the *ezo-matsu* (Yesso Spruce), etc., such shoots are pinched back with a bit left at the base. Unless removed while they are young, these shoots will become so tough as to necessitate the use of shears. Such trees as the *sugi* (Japanese Cedar), the *nezu* (Needle

Ume (Japanese Apricot)

Juniper) and *shimpaku* (Chinese Juniper), never cease to put out new shoots from spring on, so one must not neglect pinching off these shoots whenever they come out.

As for deciduous trees, such as the *kaede* (Maple), the *keyaki* (Keaki) and the *nire* (Japanese Elm), the shoots are usually nipped off, leaving two buds behind at the base, the object being to promote a dense growth of fine twigs. This pruning in a period of vigorous growth stimulates the pruned twigs to further shooting from the leaf-axils. These shoots have to be cut off, too. This process goes on till the bonsai develops into a fine shape with a graceful periphery suggestive of a grove.

The same method is not used with trees like the *ume-modoki* (Ilex serrata var. Sieboldii) and the *sanzashi* (Chinese Hawthorn), which bear small fruit. Their shoots must not be pruned off, lest they lose their flower-buds for the year. The important thing is to let such trees bear their shoots as they please and then to clip off all unnecessary twigs, leaving the flower-buds behind.

Umemodoki
(Ilex serrata var. Sieboldii)

Height : 1 ft. 5 in.

THE STUFF THAT BONSAI
ARE MADE OF

A glance at a map of Japan shows that it is an island country stretching crescent-like from north to south with a chain of mountains running through it like a ridge-pole. Because of the great differences in latitude and altitude in Japan, therefore, her flora is extremely rich in variety. From level country right up to the mountain tops the entire land boasts an unlimited diversity of vegetation. Indeed Japan is one of the countries that are noted for their numerous species of plants. In some northern regions the snow and wind have combined to stunt the growth of plants, often producing a tree which remains a pigmy only about a foot tall even after scores of years has passed, a pocket edition of an aged giant in its natural state. It is these specimens that bonsai cultivators go out to collect even in the face of dangers. A few of the species that make the best of such material for bonsai are the *goyo-matsu* (Five-needled Pine), the *shim-paku* (Chinese Juniper), the *shakunage* (Rhododendron), the *tohi* (Hondo Spruce), the *todo-matsu* (Sakhalin Fir), the *hai-matsu* (Dwarf Siberian Pine), the *takane-zakura* (Prunus nipponica), the *karamatsu* (Japanese Larch obtusum), etc. Nor are these all. Some of the age-old stunted trees are found growing in cramped spaces in fissures or cavities in rocks on alpine mountains or on

Ezo-matsu (Yesso Spruce)   *Height: 2 ft. 3 in.*

Oto (Cherry)

wind-swept coasts.

It is easy to imagine the difficulty which experts experience in turning such material into bonsai. The task is great and the duties manifold. To begin with, there is often danger to be faced in seeking for suitable materials. And stunted growth and old age are not the only requisites of a good bonsai. If such specimens do not have grace and beauty, they are not worth the trouble of being dug up. Really excellent material for a bonsai masterpiece is very rare: one plant in a thousand is the usual proportion. But when found this rarity of rarities becomes a priceless bonsai in the hands of a past master of the art. Suppose such good material to work on has been procured. The next difficulty is to make such a plant take root properly, for too often such plants lose the best part of their roots when dug out. The more ancient the plant is, the greater the hazards in its successful rooting. The first thing to do when the right material is brought in is to plant it in sandy loam containing little organic matter and to put up a shelter to keep off the sun and the wind. At night the shelter must be taken away to expose the prospective bonsai to the dew, while the foliage must be sprinkled with watetr during the daytime. Thus tended, the plants should take root.

Of the majority of trees trained into bonsai, two varieties, the *goyo-matsu* (Five-needled Pine) and the *shimpaku* (Chinese Juniper) are collected in mountainous country. The *ezo-matsu* (Yesso Spruce) and the *todomatsu* (Sakhalin Fir) used to be obtained in one of the

Kurile Islands, while from Korea there used to come good specimens of the *Chosen-yamazakura* (Korean Mountain Cherry), the *tsuge* (Boxwood), and the *onko* (Japanese Yew).

Generally speaking, any kind of tree is capable of being trained into a bonsai, the only stipulation being that they should have small leaves and dense twigs. Such trees as the platanus and the magnolia have this drawback, that as bonsai their trunk, leaves and flowers lack the proper proportion.

Methods of Obtaining Bonsai Material

The usual methods of obtaining bonsai material to work on are (1) by planting cuttings, (2) by grafting, (3) by layers (4) by seedlings.

CUTTINGS

Cuttings planted by bonsai cultivators are exactly the same as those which horticulturists generally use for purposes of propagation. When a bonsai with a stout trunk is needed the thick branch of some species of tree is picked for cutting. For instance, the branches of such trees as the willow, the ivy, the *aogiri* (Parasol Tree), the maidenhair tree and the *umemodoki* (Ilex serrata var. Sieboldii), measuring even one inch across will take root, when planted as cuttings with judicious care and skill. For baby bonsai fine twigs are usually chosen as cuttings.

GRAFTING

In bonsai culture grafting is not often resorted to.

Yanagi (Weeping Willow)

This is because the joint where the twig is grafted on to the stock usually remains visible. But grafting methods have improved so much lately that in some cases the joint is hardly noticeable. In bonsai ideal grafting should leave little or no mark at all to show where the scion is inserted on the stock.

Root-Grafting. In root-grafting a root is grafted on to the shapely twig cut off a tree for the purpose of creating a separate tree. This method is sometimes used with the *ume* (Japanese Apricot), the cherry and the pine trees.

LAYERAGE

This is a process by which the upper part of a stem or a branch is induced to take root. When it has rooted, the stem or the branch, as the case may be, is cut off. The first process is to bind with a piece of wire the part where the parent plant is expected to root. The idea is to stop the sap from flowing downward. Then the section is wrapped up with earth or sphagnum. Sometimes the section is ring-barked to stimulate it to take root. When the desired result is obtained, the portion is cut off from the parent tree and planted in a pot. This method is usually adopted as a short cut when one wants a tree with a thick stem.

SEEDLINGS

It is a slow process to raise a plant from seed and gradually train it into a bonsai of the first order. But nevertheless it is a gratifying task, though it demands no

Momi (Momi Fir)

Height: 2 ft. 8 in.

Suishi-kaido
(Hall Crab)

little patience. Many a first-rate bonsai has, in fact, been raised from seed.

Chief among the trees that can be grown from seed are the *keyaki* (Keaki), the maple-tree, the *aogiri* (Parasol·Tree), the *haze* (Japanese Wax Tree), the *kuri* (Japanese Chestnut), the *icho* (Maidenhair Tree), and the *matsu* (Pine). For the first two or three years the seedlings are grown in clusters, and are then separated and trained into bonsai.

TRIMMING PROSPECTIVE BONSAI INTO SHAPE

Few of the trees or shrubs pulled out of the garden or collected from the fields or mountains are so well shaped that they need not be trimmed or dwarfed before they can make good bonsai. Here is where the art of the bonsai maker comes in. But nanization must be conducted so as to leave few or no traces. The two principal "don'ts" in bonsai culture are: (1) Don't leave traces of the place where the top of the trunk or branches are lopped off; and (2) don't bend or twist the stem or branches unnaturally.

I repeat that there was a time when a group of bonsai fanciers favored specimens of unnatural shape, the abnormalities of which they emphasized to give the impression that they were freaks of nature. Today, however, that is no longer true, because the tendency is to respect naturalness.

The usual way to bend a stem or a branch is to wind a wire round it spirally. It is the spiral that keeps the branch in the desired shape. The wire is taken off from six to twelve months later, but the branch so bent will keep the desired shape.

In Japan there is a group of artisans whose business it is to trim bonsai into shape at the request of bonsai lovers. Such is the dexterity these experts show in per-

Ringo (Apple)

forming what seem to be impossibilities that we may be justified in asserting that bonsai culture is an art.

In bonsai culture trimming aims not so much at symmetry as at the beauty of balance hidden in a seeming unsymmetry. Trees in their natural state are seldom symmetrical in shape. In bonsai, as in Japanese landscape gardening and flower arrangement (*ikebana*), the canons of aesthetic taste dictate a beauty that comes from a studied violation of symmetry.

POTS FOR BONSAI

Pots are to bonsai what frames are to pictures. The picture frame sets off to advantage the painting which it encloses. The loveliest bonsai would be unpleasant to the eye if the pot it is planted in is not suitable. The tree and the pot must blend to make a harmonious whole, if the creator would have it be a thing of beauty. Lack of harmony there will detract much from the intrinsic value of a bonsai.

As in garments and shoes, size and style in a pot demand important consideration. Just as a child's shoes would never fit the feet of a grownup, or conversely an adult's shoes would look absurd on a child, so the relationship between plant and pot in a bonsai. No matter how lovely in color and style a bonsai pot may be, if it overwhelms or overshadows the plant, it is not suitable for the purpose. The important thing in a pot is that it must help bring out the beauty, elegance, or sublimity of the tree.

Every bonsai tree must have a pot that suits it. A new one fresh from the kiln does not harmonize with a tree bearing the aura of age, any more than does an antique pot with a sapling. The same is true in regard to the shape and form. Deep, shallow, round, oblong, square, rectangular, and diamond-shaped pots—all these have their uses. One type of pot will do for all kinds of

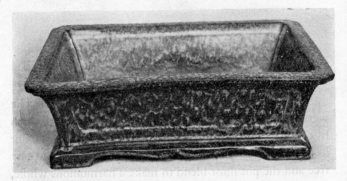

A bonsai pot

tulips, but different bonsai trees require different types of pots according to their form, size and shape.

Pots of gorgeous color are not appropriate for bonsai cultivation. Since the object of a bonsai is to suggest a landscape, the color of the pot should be symbolic of the earth or of rocks. For this purpose pots in quiet colors like dark brown, gray, black, dark red and dark purple are commonly chosen. Here, as in other branches of Japanese art, sobriety is the keynote. It seems that the average horticulturist does not give as careful consideration to the colors and shapes of flower-pots as do the devotees of bonsai culture. Appreciation of the beautiful as expressed by the Japanese is characterized by a love of subdued effects. The Japanese aesthete often uses such untranslatable words as *sabi* and *wabi*, which can best be explained as the reverse of garish and gaudy, a condition suggesting the mellowed patina of age. One of the factors in elegance of pots or trays used for

Different types of bonsai pots (1)

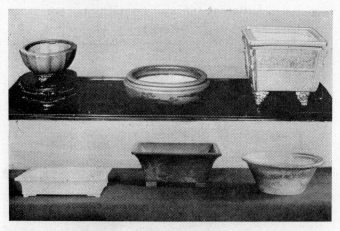

Different types of bonsai pots (2)

bonsai is soberness of colors. Ancient patinated pots are in keeping with aged trees cultivated as bonsai. But antique pots do not harmonize with seedlings or saplings full of youth and vigor. For such trees and plants glazed pots or newly baked unglazed pots may be used to advantage.

To produce the healthiest plants in bonsai culture, it is best to use unglazed pottery, but as these are not very artistic, rough pottery baked at a temperature of about 1,000°C. is usually substituted. Formerly products from the pottery center in the Iking area in China were most popular with exacting bonsai cultivators, but in recent years substitutes for the Iking products have been turned out in Japanese kilns.

Mention has already been made of the shallow trays

sometimes used with trees and sometimes without them. These trays always have water in them, so they are much shallower than those used in flower arrangements. Since these shallow bonsai trays are designed to suggest an expanse of water like the sea or a lake, they must be chosen with great attention to their shapes and colors.

A tray-like bonsai pot

TREES FOR BONSAI

(1) Trees of the Genus of **Pines**

Trees of this genus occupy first place among bonsai. There are many species including the *kuro-matsu* or Japanese black pine, the *aka-matsu,* or Japanese red pine, the *goyo-matsu* (Five-needled Pine), the *oba-goyomatsu* (Korean Pine), the *hai-matsu* (Dwarf Siberian Pine).

Kuro-matsu (Japanese Black Pine)

Most of the kuro-matsu trained into bonsai are selected from among those growing on sandy hills or on the rocks along a wind-swept coast. At present a great many specimens come from islands in the Inland Sea. The trunks of these trees are usually vigorous and masculine, and often gnarled. The only drawback is that their needles are too long to be in harmony with the size of the branches and the trunk.

In planting a pine in a pot the usual practice is to mix equal quantities of soil and sand and place the tree firmly in the mixture. Sometimes nothing but sand is used for the purpose. The tree thus planted need not be transplanted more than once in five years. To prevent overgrowth the new shoots are generally pinched off two or threee inches from the base before they develop fully into needles. There is no need for winter protection. A little manure given twice a year—in spring and autumn—is all that is necessary.

This shimpaku (Chinese Juniper) bonsai was exhibited at the
1937 Paris International Exposition of Arts and Techniques
and won the grand prize.

Zakuro
(Pomegranate)

Height: 1 ft. 8 in.

Aka-matsu (Japanese Red Pine)

This species rarely grows in coastal areas, but is found widely in mountainous country and in the fields. In fact there is hardly any landscape in Japan but what is dotted with clusters of this pine-tree. As its name implies, this species is marked by its reddish brown trunk. As a bonsai this tree is prized for its elegance. One of its drawbacks is, however, its low resistance to the harmful effect of smoke. When kept in town, *aka-matsu* bonsai should be cleansed with water morning and evening. The method followed in cultivating this tree is much the same as that used with the *kuro-matsu*.

Goyo-matsu (Five-needled Pine)

No other species of the Pinus genus is more popular with bonsai gardeners than the goyo-matsu. This species also makes the best bonsai. Its slender twigs and short needles harmonize admirably with the miniature trunk. Furthermore, it is generally regarded as easiest to cultivate. This tree is to be found throughout the country at an altitude of about 2,300 ft. above sea level. Specimens made from dwarfs found on these open spaces growing on little patches of earth left on a cliff or in a fissure in a rock are valued highly. Some bonsai are obtained from seedlings, and others from grafting as in the olden days. Those with branches bent in the shape of a series of S's arranged in a row show that they were trained in the days when grafting was the rule.

The *goyo-matsu* is cultivated in the same way as the aforesaid *kuro-matsu*, but as its natural habitat is the mist-covered highlands care should be taken to water

Both of the plants on these pages are examples of the
Kuro-matsu (Japanese Black Pine), but differ so greatly in
appearance because of their different places of origin and
methods of cultivation

~ 135

its leaves both in the morning and evening.

Hai-matsu (Dwarf Siberian Pine)

This is a creeping alpine species of pine found growing on peaks some 10,000 ft. above sea level. These pines are very difficult subjects to train into bonsai.

Goyo-matsu (Five-needled Pine) with three trunks growing from one stump   *Height: 1 ft. 7 in.*

Oba-goyo-matsu (Korean Pine)

This tree has long needles, and its bark is not as deeply marked by scaly indentations as are the other species of the pine. For these reasons this tree is seldom used for bonsai.

San-yo-sho (American Three-needled Pine)

This tree is indigenous to the United States of America and not very plentiful in this country. As it makes a good bonsai, it is popular with bonsai cultivators and possibilities are that this kind of bonsai will become still more popular in the future. Favorite characteristics of these bonsai are (1) its trunk resembles that of the *kuro-matsu* (Japanese Black Pine), (2) its needles are shorter than those of the *kuro-matsu* and are in good proportion with its trunk and branches; and (3) its leaves grow from its trunk and branches. Unlike most other species of the pine, this particular kind puts forth shoots at the base of a twig when its tip is pruned, which is an important factor in checking the overgrowth of branches. All in all, this American species of pine-tree has the makings of fine bonsai.

(2) **Sakura** (Cherry-tree)

The charm of a cherry bonsai, standing about a foot high and resplendent with blossoms, used as an interior ornament cannot be equalled. As a bonsai the cherry is one of the most highly prized flowering trees in Japan.

There are some three hundred or more species of *sakura*, and these may be roughly divided into two classes: the *yamazakura* (Mountain Cherry) and the *satozakura* (Japanese Flowering Cherry). The latter include more than 200 species cultivated by horticulturists, and their blossoms at their best are breath-taking in their loveliness. But it is the former that is more prized as bonsai; for in bonsai the cherry-tree is admired not so much for its flowers as for its shapeliness.

A cherry-tree bonsai blooms one or two weeks earlier than its cousins growing in their natural state. The species known as the *taiwan-hizakura* (Prunus campanulata), one of the mountain cherry trees, blooms in early spring, followed by others such as the *higanzakura* (Drooping Cherry) and *fujizakura* (Prunus incisa). Then toward the middle of April come the trees at the cherry blossom resorts so familiar to all beauty lovers.

The cherry is one of the most difficult trees to cultivate as bonsai. It has to be transplanted once a year, generally immediately after the blossoms have fallen. The old loam in the pot must be replaced by new. Half of the roots have to be cut off. The new soil should contain 30 per cent leaf mold. The cherry bonsai is usually given liquid manure or fertilizer in powdered form once a week from May right up to October.

Yamazakura (Mountain Cherry)

A 200-year old ezo-matsu
(Yesso Spruce)

Height: 1 ft. 9 in.
Photographed in January

Pruning should be done very sparingly in the cultivation of cherry trees. There is a Japanese saying which states "He is a fool who prunes cherry trees; so is he who does not prune the *ume* (Japanese Apricot)." Never prune more branches of the cherry tree than you can help.

(3) **Ezo-matsu** (Yesso Spruce)

The principal source of the *ezo-matsu* bonsai in the past was in the damp moors on one of the Kurile Islands. These moors are covered with moss and the soil is acid; in fact no other trees can possibly grow there. The robust ezo-matsu can sprout on such land and grow, but it is stunted by the snow and wind. It was these dwarf trees that were collected for bonsai cultivation.

The very short needle-leaves of this tree grow in clusters on twigs in correct proportion with the trunk and boughs, while the little trunk appears like that of an aged tree. This is its main attraction as a bonsai.

Because of its hardiness, this tree can easily be trained into a bonsai. It is cultivated pretty much in the same way as the pine-tree; only that it has to be transplanted once every two or three years. The new shoots are pinched off near the base, while they are nice and tender. No special winter protection is necessary. This bonsai does not need manuring more than twice a year—in spring and autumn—but has to be watered sufficiently from time to time.

(4) Ume (Japanese Apricot)

The Japanese are very fond of the pine-tree, the cherry-tree and the Japanese Apricot. At New Year's the usual practice in Japan is to place a *ume* bonsai in the living-room as an ornament. Such a bonsai is necessarily given special stimulation to encourage early blooming. *Ume* bonsai are esteemed for the fact that they put forth fragrant blossoms in the early spring when freezing weather still prevails throughout the country.

From ancient times it has been said that there are something like 500 species of the *ume*, but in all probability there are no more than 200 distinguishable from one another.

Time was when old, stunted *ume* trees were found growing wild on rocky hills. These "wild plum-trees," as they were called, were highly prized by bonsai cultivators. But today there are no longer any to be found. Most of the *ume* bonsai of today are obtained either from seedlings, cuttings or grafts, or by means of the dwarfing of larger trees.

Ume bonsai require annual transplantation, usually soon after the blooming season is over. At the same time the shoots are cut off at the base, leaving only two buds.

The loam used in the transplantation of *ume* bonsai should contain about 10 per cent of leaf mold and 20 per cent of sand. Manure is given once a week from April to May, and then twice a month from October to November.

(5) Kaki (Japanese Persimmon)

In this country persimmon trees bearing fruit are so common a sight in the rural districts in the fall that autumn is often called persimmon autumn. It is indeed pleasant to see the fruit left hanging from the twigs like so many big vermilion gems, when the tinted leaves start falling off the trees.

Persimmon trees when used as bonsai ,are supposed to suggest such charming rural scenes. When properly cultivated, these bonsai bear fruit abundantly. Ordinary-sized fruit hanging from the pigmy bonsai must surprise the uninitiated, and they are definitely out of proportion to the foliage. For this reason bonsai fanciers usually prefer the *yamagaki*, a sort of wild persimmon

K a k i (Japanese Persimmon) —Succulent fruit has already been plucked and eaten from this prolific tree

tree, which bears tiny little fruit about the size of a comparatively small date.

(6) **Sugi** (Japanese Cedar)

The *sugi* is generally considered to be indigenous to Japan. A somewhat similar species grows, it is said, in Darjeeling, India. There are extensive *sugi* forests here and there throughout the country; the famous avenues of these trees at Nikko and Hakone, or groves ubiquitous in Japanese temple and shrine precincts greet the eyes of every visitor to these shores. Centuries old, these giant cedars stand majestically and sublime with the green of their foliage blending harmoniously with the vermilion of the shrine buildings which nestle amongst them. *Sugi* bonsai are intended to give us the same impression that we get from these trees in their natural habitat. But it is difficult to obtain from a bonsai the feeling of sublimity which these aged giants so invariably produce in us.

The *sugi* tree grows well in damp ground, and where the air has a high percentage of humidity, and dislikes the sort of dry air which prevails on a continent. In all probability, therefore, this tree, whether as a bonsai or not, would not thrive satisfactorily out of Japan.

(7) **Buna** (Japanese Beech)

One characteristic of this tree is its trunk which is the color of oxidized silver and another is the way it stands in winter, keeping dry leaves on the twigs. The dead leaves do not fall off the tree till late spring, when the new shoots with their whitish green appear. So when

Sugi (Japanese Cedar) cultivated on a flat stone

we look at this tree in late spring we are reminded of autumn, and the sight, not too common a one, is in its own way rather interesting. This tree never branches more than once a year. It is so robust that it grows in any soil. It can survive existence in a tray containing water, or in a pot sparingly supplied with water. Indeed, the *buna* is a very good example of a bonsai as a symbol of austerity, which I believe a good bonsai should be.

(8) **Umemodoki** (Ilex serrata var. Sieboldii)

The lustrous, coral-like fruit of this tree, as it hangs

from the branches, is as charming as any cluster of flowers, and even more so. As the weather gets more and more frosty, the tinted leaves fall to the ground, but the pretty berries of the umemodoki lend their charm to the otherwise desolate scene all winter long up to the following year. This tree is a favorite as a bonsai because pruning makes it more luxuriant in a pot than in its natural state and keeps its branches in good shape.

The secret of making this bonsai bear well consists in stimulating the growth of its roots, forcing them to grow as quickly as possible in summer. The idea is to make the bonsai root-bound and thereby suppress further growth of the tree. Thus stimulated, the plant will bloom and bear well. The same method is used with *ume* (Japanese Apricot) and the *zakuro* (Pomegranate).

Buna (Japanese Beech) with
two trunks growing from one
stump

Photographed in January

Umemodoki

(Ilex serrata var. Sieboldii)

Photographed

in December

(9) Zakuro (Pomegranate)

When the flowers of spring fade and are followed by the verdant leafage of early summer, this is one of the few trees that still bear scarlet blossoms among a mass of green. This striking contrast is most agreeable to the eye.

Some fifty years ago there was a great vogue in Japan for pomegranate blossoms. Scores of new varieties were developed by the horticulturists in those days, and these caught the fancy of the masses. Today, however, they are not as popular. The pomegranate bonsai of today are mostly relics of these days; living legacies full of the ancient reminders of a passing fad.

The method of cultivating this tree is different from that used with most other trees. As the original home of the pomegranate is along the Mediterranean where a mild climate prevails, the plant is liable to be adversely affected by cold weather. For this reason it is customary to keep pomegranate bonsai in a room maintaining temperatures from zero to 10°C during the winter, so as to prevent the soil from freezing. At the same time care must be taken to keep the air from getting too dry. For pomegranate bonsai often die from excessive dryness, as well as from cold.

What has been said of the *ume* (Japanese Apricot) in relation to the soil and its fertilizers applies also to the pomegranate. For transplanting, the best time is in the late spring when the tree begins to bud. Precautions must be taken against excessive bearing. It is essential to keep the tree bearing in moderation, for exhaustion

Zakuro
(Pomegranate)

Photographed in July

from excessive bearing sometimes proves fatal. The same thing may be said of other fruit-bearing bonsai such as the *kaki* (Japanese Persimmon) and the maiden-hair tree.

A pomegranate baby bonsai

Height: 7 in.

(10) Shimpaku (Chinese Juniper)

The *shimpaku* which is commonly trained into a bonsai is a sort of shrub to be found in mountains about 3,000 ft. above sea level. Of all the bonsai, the *shimpaku* is admired most because of its shapely outline.

The loam used in the cultivation of this bonsai is much the same as that used for the pine-tree, only it is not pressed down so firmly when the tree is planted. Transplantation is done once in every three years. One must also remember to manure the bonsai regularly from spring to autumn. As the cord-like leaves of this tree grow from spring to autumn, it is necessary to pinch off the overgrown leaves with the fingers to encourage the growth of new leaves, making the tips of the twigs thick and bushy.

(11) Yanagi (Willow tree)

The willow trees with their fresh leaves take the most prominent place among the trees of spring. They are a proverbial harbinger of spring for the urban people in Japan. They remind the practical-minded of the useful willow wands and the timber they yield, and make men of taste dream to themselves of their downy flowers in spring and their drooping branches swaying this way and that in the summer breeze.

The species most prized by bonsai fanciers is the one called *rokkakudo-yanagi*, the most notable feature of which is its drooping foliage, its branches sometimes being more than 15 ft. long. This type of willow grows along the banks of the Kamo which flows through the

Shimpaku (Chinese Juniper)

Yanagi
(Weeping Willow)

Photographed in April

154 ~

city of Kyoto. Even in a bonsai the branches sometimes grow as long as six feet, a fact which makes it necessary to place the pot high so that the cascading strips of green may be seen to advantage from below.

The willow is a plant of such vigorous growth that by summer the roots of a bonsai will permeate every part of the soil renewed at the time of spring transplantation and absorb all the nourishment contained in the soil. When pot-bound roots cannot absorb any nutrition, no matter what fertilizer is used, the plant will not be able to stand the cold. The thing to do in such a case is to pull the tree out of the pot toward the end of August, break up the matted roots, prune off about one-third of them and replant the tree in the pot. By the end of autumn the roots will have reached every part of the tray, so vigorous is the growth of the willow. All the shoots are cut off at their base toward the end of spring, but by summer the tree will be full of drooping shoots again.

(12) Momiji (Maple tree)

The most representative of the deciduous trees whose leaves change in color in the fall is the maple-tree. When the whole countryside is ablaze it is the maple trees that stand out conspicuously in all their splendor. The shoots of this tree are scarlet when they first appear in spring, and then they gradually turn green. This change of color from red to green is as great a feast to the eye as the autumnal tints. And again the maple tree in leaf is as pretty as when it is stripped of leaves in winter. In other words, this tree presents a kaleidoscope of color and charm through the four seasons of the year. This is why the maple gains the favor of bonsai cultivators.

No particular care is required in the cultivation of this bonsai. The tree does not need to be transplanted more than once in two years. As this tree puts out shoots vigorously from spring right on to early summer, these must be pinched off at the base, leaving only one or two knots behind. This will stimulate a further ramification of branches. There are many species of the maple. Those which are chosen for bonsai culture should have, as far as possible, these characteristics to be marked by: (1) comparatively small leaves, (2) deeply divided leaves (3) shoots of a bright color, and (4) autumnal tints of a deep color.

(13) Tsubaki (Camellia)

There are more than 200 species of camellia. For gardens and interior decoration those with large double blossoms are generally preferred, but for bonsai purposes the wild camellia which has small, single-petalled blossoms is considered more suitable.

Then there are species with snow-white or small light pink flowers which are often used for flower arrangements in a ceremonial tea room. The species which has white flowers is called *shiratama-tsubaki* and the one with little light pink flowers *wabisuke*.

The cultivation of camellia trees as bonsai requires some attention. As the roots of this tree tend to harden the soil in the pot in which it is planted, annual transplantation is necessary and the soil should contain some 30% of leaf mold. The time for transplantation is in the middle of April, as in the case of most other evergreens. Furthermore, the trees must be manured regularly little by little, as it demands much nourishment.

(14) **Take** (Bamboo)

Bonsai experts plant a cluster of little bamboo trees in a pot only about an inch deep and cultivate them in such a way that young bamboo shoots will emerge from underground stems year in and year out, thereby suggesting a luxuriant bamboo grove growing to a height of some 60 ft. One may think this almost impossible to achieve, but experts in the art of bonsai culture often succeed in attaining the next to impossible.

Mosochiku (Moso Bamboo)

Kanchiku
(Winter
Bamboo)

There is hardly any kind of bamboo but is amenable to bonsai cultivation. But it is no easy task to train bamboo into a bonsai. We shall therefore confine ourselves to giving a few hints on how to look after bamboo bonsai. Bamboo roots usually grow to great lengths. In the case of a bamboo bonsai, the roots will go round and round along the wall of the pot till they get completely matted. If left in that condition, the plant will weaken and eventually wither away. So it must be transplanted every year just before the young shoots appear. If transplanted too early, the plant is liable to be damaged by the cold, if too late, the young shoots in the process of development are likely to be hurt. For this reason the middle of April is generally considered just about the right time for transplantation.

First of all, take the plant out of the pot and cut off part of the matted roots. Next, break up the tangled roots and prune away about half of the original roots, and replace the old soil with fresh. In pruning the roots the bonsai gardener must keep the future contour of the plant in mind as he pares off the unwanted shoot-to-be already visible on the main roots.

The bamboo is a moisture-loving plant, and so it does not matter how often it is watered, so long as the pot is provided with proper drain-holes. In fertilizing use a little manure frequently.

When placed in an ill-ventilated room, a bamboo bonsai is liable to be affected by noxious insects. It is not advisable to keep the plant under direct sunlight all day in the summer. It should be kept away from the sun in the afternoon from three o'clock on.

(15) **Fuji** (Japanese Wistaria)

One of the prettiest wild flowers found in mountainous country in the early summer is the *yama-fuji* or wild wistaria. It is often found in bloom amidst the fresh foliage halfway down a precipice, within reach of none but birds and monkeys. Sometimes this plant entwines itself round an arbor-tree and, making its way up, crowns the latter with pretty flowers. As a bonsai, the wistaria

Fuji (Japanese wistaria)   *Photographed in July*

Satsuki (Satsuki Azalea)   *Photographed in June*

162 ～

blooms quite well, its clusters of flowers sometimes being as long as two feet. As a rule, the wistaria likes damp soil, but there is a species known as the *okanoda* which also thrives in dry districts. It is this latter species which is usually adapted to bonsai culture.

The wistaria requires a lot of water. When frequent watering is inconvenient, the plant is left, pot and all, in a tray containing water, so that half the pot is immersed. Also, plenty of manure must be given a wistaria bonsai to make it bear many flowers. The tree has to be transplanted once every year in the spring.

(16) **Tsutsuji** (Azalea)

There are numerous species of tsutsuji. Chief among those commonly cultivated by bonsai horticulturists are the *kirishima* (Rhododendron), the *satsuki* (Satsuki Azalea) and the *ryukyu* (Rhododendron mucronatum).

The azalea so popular these days in Japan is the second of these, the *satsuki*. It is said that there are as many as 500 varieties of this species. In the feudal days of the Tokugawa shogunate more than 100 species were already in cultivation. There are so many varieties of the wild azalea that they cannot be enumerated here.

The azalea is recommended to any one who wishes to try his hand at bonsai, because it is about the easiest of any plant to cultivate as a bonsai.

(17) **Saifuriboku** (Juneberry)

Like the American dogwood this plant puts forth a mass of tiny little white flowers, which give the effect from a distance of a bush covered with snow. There is a recent tendency among bonsai cultivators to grow this kind of tree merely for its flowers that can be appreciated equally from all sides.

(18) **Nezu** (Needle Juniper)

This tree is prized for its majestic trunk and its fine, short leaves which remain green throughout the four seasons. Some varieties have fine, long needles and creeping trunks. Illustrated on page 166 is one of these varieties trained into a bonsai.

Dry air is disastrous to a potted *nezu*. However moist its root may be, the tree will lose its green leaves, if the air is dry. Overgrown shoots should be constantly pinched off, as the tree keeps on putting out shoots from spring right on to early autumn.

Saifuriboku
(Juneberry)

Photographed in April

Nezu (Needle Juniper)

APPENDIX

WHERE TO SEE BONSAI

(1) TOKYO BONSAI CLUB

Address: Ikenohata, Ueno Park, Taito-ku, Tokyo.

Phone Number: Shitaya (83) 8783.

Access: The Club is located on the northwest shore of Lake Shinobazu in Ueno Park. Take street-car No. 37 and get off at the Ikenohata-shi-chikencho car stop. The Club is just opposite the car stop across a narrow street.

The Tokyo Bonsai Club was founded by a group of bonsai gardeners and dealers who wished to display their bonsai to the public. Every month an exhibition of bonsai—sometimes trees of the pine genus, sometimes flowering plants, and sometimes various kinds of trees—is held at the Club. At other times visitors may see bonsai displayed in the Club gardens and get help and information from the manager of the Club. Bonsai are also on sale at the exhibitions held at the Club.

(2) Besides the above-mentioned Club, there are many first-rate bonsai shops in Tokyo and other parts of the country which are worth visiting. More detailed information about these shops may be obtained from the Tokyo Bonsai Club.

(3) The villages and cities listed below have long been famous as being the haunts of bonsai enthusiasts, though there may be some changes in them now due to the vicissitudes of war and time.

    (1) Bonsai-mura, Omiya, Saitama prefecture.

    (2) Hashioka-mura, Ayauta-gun, Kagawa prefecture.

    (3) Koi-machi, Hiroshima, Hiroshima prefecture.

    (4) Komoto-cho, Nakagawa-ku, Nagoya, Aichi prefecture.

    (5) Matsumoto, Nagano prefecture.

    (6) Nagao-mura, Kawabe-gun, Hyogo prefecture.

MAGAZINE ON BONSAI

"BONSAI," a monthly magazine in Japanese, edited by Norio Kobayashi and published by the Kusamura-kai Society, Ako, Kami-Inagun, Nagano Prefecture, Japan. $1.70 a year including postage.

INDEX

(1) List of Trees (In Japanese)

(2) List of Trees (In English)

— A —

American Three-needled Pine (Amerika san-yosho), 137

Apple (Ringo), 47, 48, 107

Apricot, Japanese (Ume), 48, 91, 94, 108, 118, 141, 142

Azalea (Tsutsuji), 47, 48, 94, 163

Azalea, Satsuki (Satsuki), 163

— B —

Bamboo (Take), 158

Bamboo, Moso (Mosochiku), 158

Bamboo, Winter (Kanchiku), 159

Beech, Japanese (Buna), 144

Black Pine (Kuro-matsu), 130

Box-thorn (Kuko), 51

Boxwood (Tsuge), 116

— C —

Cedar, Japanese (Sugi), 82, 100, 108, 144

Celastrus articulatus (Tsuru-umemodoki), 51

Cherry (Sakura), 47, 108, 118, 138

Cherry (Oto), 47

Chestnut, Japanese (Kuri), 121

Chinese Hawthorn (Sanzashi), 47, 110

Chinese Juniper (Shimpaku), 57, 59, 93, 110, 112, 115, 152

Common Reed (Ashi), 69

Crab-Apple, Kaido (Kaido), 47, 48

Cypress, Hinoki (Hinoki), 17

— D —

Date Plum (Mamegaki), 51

Dog Rose, Japanese (Nobara), 42, 48

Dogwood (Hanamizuki), 163

Dogwood, Japanese (Yamaboshi), 51

Drooping Cherry (Higan-zakura), 138

Dwarf Bamboo (Sasa), 69

Dwarf Siberian Pine (Haimatsu), 112, 136

— E —

Elm, Japanese (Nire), 42, 82, 110

— F —

Fern (Shida), 69

Five-needled Pine (Goyo-matsu) 57, 112, 115, 133

Flowering Cherry, Japanese (Sato-zakura), 138

— G —

Garden Camellia (Tsubaki), 47, 157

Golden Bells (Rengyo), 47

Grape Vine (Budo), 107

Grass Sweet Flag (Sekisho), 69

172 ~

174 ～

(3) General Information

BONSAI—Miniature Potted Trees
（盆　　栽）

昭和二十五年　十　月二十四日初版発行
昭和二十六年　九　月　十五日再版発行
昭和二十七年　六　月二十五日三版発行
昭和二十七年十一月二十五日四版発行

著者検印
省　略

定價參百五拾円

著　者　　小　林　憲　雄
発行人　　入　沢　文　明

東京都千代田区丸ノ内一ノ一
発行所　　日　本　交　通　公　社
（振替東京　29403）

東京都板橋区志村町五番地
印刷所　　凸　版　印　刷　株　式　会　社

Published by JAPAN TRAVEL BUREAU
PRICE:　¥ 350
Printed in Japan, 1952

266-E 114　T 13 IV-0552